MOTHER
GOOSE'S
NURSERY
RHYMES

TO THE
QUEEN

Introduction.

"MAY I have the pleasure to introduce
Some very old friends?" says Mother Goose.

"There's little Bo-Peep and little Boy Blue,
The little old Woman who lived in a shoe,

Old Mother Hubbard as well as her dog,
Dame Trot and Sir Anthony Rowley Frog,

Humpty Dumpty, and Dickory Dock,
The dear little mouse who ran up the clock,

The puss who journeyed to London alone,
And saw the queen on a golden throne:

So come, my little folks, open me,
And lots of other old friends you'll see!"

There was a Little Man.

THERE was
a little man,
And he had
a little gun,
And his bullets
were made
of lead, lead, lead;
He went to the brook,
And saw a little duck,
And shot it through
the head, head, head.
He carried it home to his old wife Joan,
And bade her a fire to make, make, make,
To roast the little duck
He had shot in the brook,
And he'd go and fetch
the drake, drake, drake.

Mother Goose's Nursery Rhymes.

Dickory, Dickory, Dock.

DICKORY, dickory, dock,
    The mouse ran up the clock,
The clock struck one,
The mouse ran down;
Hickory, dickory, dock.

There was an Old Man.

THERE was an old man,
And he had a calf,
    And that's half;
He took him out of the stall,
And put him on the wall,
    And that's all.

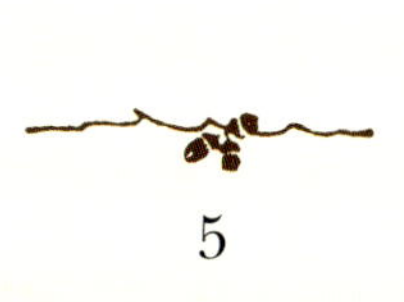

There Was a Crooked Man.

THERE was a crooked man, and he went a crooked mile,
He found a crooked sixpence against a crooked stile:
he bought a crooked cat, which caught a crooked mouse,
And they all lived together in a little crooked house.

Little Bo-Peep.

LITTLE Bo-peep has lost her sheep,
    And can't tell where to find them;
Leave them alone, and they'll come home,
    And bring their tails behind them.

Little Bo-peep fell fast asleep,
    And dreamed she heard them bleating;
But when she awoke, she found it a joke,
    For they were still a-fleeting.

Then up she took her little crook,
    Determined for to find them;
She found them indeed,
    But it made.her heart bleed,
For they'd left all their tails behind 'em.

Peter Piper.

PETER PIPER picked a peck of pickled peppers;
A peck of pickled peppers Peter Piper picked;
If Peter Piper picked a peck of pickled peppers,
Where's the peck of pickled peppers Peter Piper picked?

Little Bo-Peep

A was an apple-pie;

B bit it;

C cut it;

D dealt it;

E eat it;

F fought for it;

G got it;

H had it;

J joined it;

K kept it;

L longed for it;

M mourned for it;

N nodded at it;

O opened it;

P peeped in it;

Q quartered it;

R ran for it;

S stole it;

T took it;

V viewed it;

W wanted it;

X, Y, Z, and Amperse-And

All wished for a piece in hand.

A Dog and a Cat
  Went Out Together.

A DOG and a cat went out together,
  To see some friends just out of town;
Said the cat to the dog,
"What d'ye think of the weather?"
"I think, ma'am, the rain will come down;
But don't be alarmed, for I've an umbrella
That will shelter us both," said this amiable fellow.

"What will the children do then, poor things?"

This is the Way.

THIS is the way the ladies ride;
   Tri, tre, tre, tree,
   Tri, tre, tre, tree!
This is the way the ladies ride,
     Tri, tre, tre, tre, tri, tre, tre, tree!

   This is the way the gentlemen ride;
     Gallop-a-trot,
     Gallop-a-trot!
   This is the way the gentlemen ride,
     Gallop-a-trot-a-trot!

   This is the way the farmers ride;
     Hobbledy-hoy,
     Hobbledy-hoy!
   This is the way the farmers ride,
     Hobbledy-hobbledy-hoy!

The North Wind.

   THE north wind doth blow,
   And we shall have snow,
   And what will the robin do then,
     Poor thing?

   He'll sit in the barn
   And keep himself warm,
   And hide his head under his wing,
     Poor thing.

The north wind doth blow,
And we shall have snow,
And what shall the honey-bee do,
            Poor thing?

In his hive he will stay
Till the cold's passed away,
And then he'll come out in the spring,
            Poor thing.

The north wind doth blow,
And we shall have snow,
And what will the dormouse do then,
            Poor thing?

Rolled up like a ball
In his nest snug and small,
He'll sleep till warm weather comes back,
            Poor thing.

The north wind doth blow,
And we shall have snow,
And what will the children do then,
            Poor things?

When lessons are done,
They'll jump, skip, and run,
And that's how they'll keep themselves warm,
            Poor things.

"The north wind doth blow."

The Old Woman and Her Pig.

AN old woman was sweeping her house, and she found a little crooked sixpence. "What," said she, "shall I do with this little sixpence? I will go to market, and buy a little pig." As she was coming home, she came to a stile; the piggy would not go over the stile.

She went a little farther, and she met a dog. So she said to the dog—

> "Dog, dog, bite pig;
> Piggy won't get over the stile;
> And I shan't get home to-night."

But the dog would not.
She went a little farther, and she met a stick. So she said—

"Stick, stick, beat dog;
Dog won't bite pig;
Piggy won't get over the stile;
And I shan't get home to-night."

But the stick would not. She went a little farther, and she met a fire. So she said—

"Fire, fire, burn stick;
Stick won't beat dog;
Dog won't bite pig;
Piggy won't get over the stile;
And I shan't get home to-night."

But the fire would not.

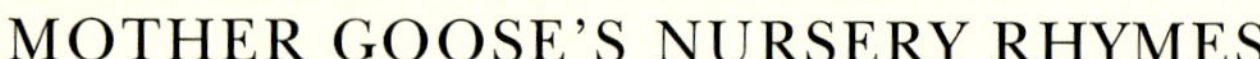

She went a little farther, and she met some water.
So she said—

> "Water, water, quench fire;
> Fire won't burn stick ;" etc.

But the water would not.

She went a little farther, and she met an Ox.
So she said—

> "Ox ox , drink water;
> Water won't quench fire;" etc.

But the ox would not.

She went a little farther and she met a butcher. So she said—

> "Butcher, butcher, kill ox;
> Ox won't drink water;" etc.

But the butcher would not. She went a little farther, and she met a rope. So she said—

> "Rope, rope, hang butcher;
> Butcher won't kill ox ;" etc.

But the rope would not. She went a little farther, and she met a rat. So she said—

> "Rat, rat gnaw rope;
> Rope won't hang butcher;" etc.

But the rat would not.
She went a little farther, and she met a cat. So she said—

> "Cat, cat, kill rat;
> Rat won't gnaw rope ;" etc.

But the cat said to her, "If you will go to yonder cow, and fetch me a saucer of milk, I will kill the rat."
So away went the old woman to the cow, and said—

> "Cow, cow, give me a saucer of milk;
> Cat won't kill rat ;" etc.

But the cow said to her, "If you will go to yonder hay-makers, and fetch me a wisp of hay, I'll give you the milk." So away went the old woman to the hay-makers, and said—

"Haymakers, give me a wisp of hay;
Cow won't give me milk ;" etc.

But the haymakers said to her, "If you will go to yonder stream, and fetch us a bucket of water, we'll give you the hay." So away the old woman went; but when she got to the stream, she found the bucket was full of holes. So she covered the bottom with pebbles, and then filled the bucket with water, and away she went back with it to the haymakers; and they gave her a wisp of hay. As soon as the cow had eaten the hay, she gave the old woman the milk; and away she went with it in a saucer to the cat. As soon as the cat had lapped up the milk;—

The cat began to kill the rat;
The rat began to gnaw the rope;
The rope began to hang the butcher;
The butcher began to kill the ox
The ox began to drink the water;
The water began to quench the fire;
The fire began to burn the stick;
The stick began to beat the dog
The dog began to bite the pig;
The pig in a fright jumped over the stile;
And so the old woman got home that night.

As Tommy Snooks.

AS Tommy Snooks and Bessy Brooks
Were walking out one Sunday,
Says Tommy Snooks to Bessy Brooks,
"To-morrow will be Monday."

As Tittymouse sat.

As Tittymouse sat in the witty to spin,
Pussy came to her and bid her good e'en.
"Oh what are you doing, my little 'oman?"
"A-spinning a doublet for my gude man."
"Then shall I come to thee and wind up thy thread?"
"Oh no, Mr. Puss, you will bite off my head."

Little Jack Horner

Little Jack Horner.

LITTLE JACK Horner
Sat in the corner,
   Eating a Christmas pie;
He put in his thumb,
And he took out a plum,
   And said, "What a good boy am I!"

If I'd as Much Money.

IF I'd as much money as I could spend;
I never would cry old chairs to mend;
Old chairs to mend, old chairs to mend;
I never would cry old chairs to mend.

If I'd as much money as I could tell;
I never would cry old clothes to sell;
Old clothes to sell, old clothes to sell;
I never would cry old clothes to sell.

Pretty John Watts.

PRETTY John Watts,
We are troubled with rats,
Will you drive them out of the house?
We have mice too, in plenty,
That feast in the pantry;
But let them stay
And nibble away
What harm in a little brown mouse?

As Little Jenny Wren.

AS little Jenny Wren
    Was sitting by the shed,
She waggled with her tail,
    And nodded with her head.
She waggled with her tail,
    And nodded with her head,
As little Jenny Wren
Was sitting by the shed.

Bow-wow, says the Dog.

Bow-wow, says the dog;
    Mew, mew, says the cat;
Grunt, grunt, goes the hog;
    And squeak goes the rat.

Tu-whu, says the owl;
    Caw, caw, says the crow;
Quack, quack, says the duck;
    And what sparrows say you know.

So, with sparrows, and owls,
    With rats, and with dogs,
With ducks, and with crows,
    With cats, and with hogs,

A fine song I have made,
    To please you, my dear;
And if it's well sung,
    'Twill be charming to hear.

I had a little Hobby Horse.

I HAD a little hobby horse,
    And it was dapple gray;
Its head was made of pea straw.
    lts tail was made of hay.
I sold it to an old woman
    For a copper groat;
And I'll not sing my song again
    Without a new coat.

When Jacky's a very Good Boy.

WHEN Jacky's a very good boy,
  He shall have cakes and a custard,
  But when he does nothing but cry,
  He shall have nothing but mustard.

Bessy Bell and Mary Gray.

BESSY BELL and Mary Gray,
  They were two bonny lasses;
They built their house upon the lea,
  And covered it with rashes.
Bessy kept the garden gate,
  And Mary kept the pantry;
Bessy always had to wait,
  While Mary lived in plenty.

Dickery, dickery, dare.

DICKERY, dickery, dare,
  The pig flew up in the air;
The man in brown soon brought him down,
  Dickery, dickery, dare.

Cross-patch, Draw the Latch.

CROSS-PATCH,
  Draw the latch,
Sit by the fire and spin;
  Take a cup,
And drink it up,
  Then call your neighbours in.

Girls and Boys Come Out to Play

GIRLS
    and boys,
come out
    to play,
The moon doth
shine as bright as day;

Leave your supper
        and leave your sleep,
And come with
        your playfellows
        into the street.

Come with a whoop,
    come with a call,
Come with good will.
    or not at all.

Up the Ladder.

> Up the ladder and down the wall,
> A halfpenny roll will serve us all.
> You find milk, and I'll find flour,
> And we'll have a pudding in half an hour.

Lend Me thy Mare.

"LEND me thy mare to ride a mile ?"
"She is lamed, leaping over a stile."
"Alack! and I must keep the fair!
I'll give thee money for thy mare."
"Oh, oh, say you so?
Money will make the mare to go!"

Little Bob Snooks.

LITTLE Bob Snooks was fond of his books,
    And loved by his usher and master;
But naughty Jack Spry, he got a black eye,
    And carries his nose in a plaster.

If You Sneeze on a Monday.

IF YOU sneeze on Monday, you sneeze for danger;
Sneeze on a Tuesday, kiss a stranger;
Sneeze on a Wednesday, sneeze for a letter;
Sneeze on a Thursday, something better;
Sneeze on a Friday, sneeze for sorrow;
Sneeze on a Saturday, see your sweetheart to-morrow.

Higglepy, Piggleby

Higglepy, Piggleby,
   My black hen,
She lays eggs
   For gentlemen;
Sometimes nine,
   And sometimes ten,
Higglepy, Piggleby,
   My black hen!

A Man went a-Hunting.

A MAN went a-hunting at Reigate,
   And wished to leap over a high gate;
Says the owner, "Go round!
   With your gun and your hound,
For you never shall jump over my gate."

I love Sixpence, Pretty Little Sixpence.

I LOVE sixpence, pretty little sixpence,
   I love sixpence better than my life;
I spent a penny of it, I spent another,
   And I took fourpence home to my wife.

Oh, my little four pence, pretty little fourpence,
   I love fourpence better than my life;
I spent a penny of it, I spent another,
   And I took twopence home to my wife.

Oh, my little twopence, my pretty little twopence,
   I love twopence better than my life;
I spent a penny of it, I spent another,
   And I took nothing home to my wife.

Oh, my little nothing, my pretty little nothing,
   What will nothing buy for my wife?
I have nothing, I spend nothing,
   I love nothing better than my wife.

The Man in the Moon.

THE man in the Moon
   Came tumbling down,
And asked his
   way to Norwich;
He went by the south,
   And burnt his mouth,
With supping cold
   pease-porridge.

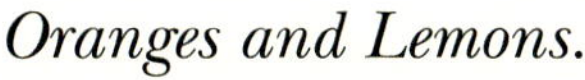

Oranges and Lemons.

GAY go up, and gay go down,
To ring the bells of London town.

Bull's eyes and targets,
Say the bells of St. Marg'ret's.

Brickbats and tiles,
Say the bells of St. Giles'.

Halfpence and farthings,
Say the bells of St. Martin's.

Oranges and lemons,
Say the bells of St. Clement's.

(continues p31)

Little Tom Tucker

LITTLE Tom Tucker

Sings for his supper;

What shall he eat?

White bread and butter.

How shall he cut it

Without e'er a knife?

How will he be married

Without e'er a wife?

Oranges and Lemons (continued from p29)

Pancakes and fritters,
Say the bells of St. Peter's.

Two sticks and an apple,
Say the bells at Whitechapel.

Old Father Baldpate,
Say the slow bells at Aldgate.

Pokers and tongs,
Say the bells at St. John's.

Kettles and pans,
Say the bells at St. Ann's.

You owe me ten shillings,
Say the bells at St. Helen's.

When will you pay me?
Say the bells at Old Bailey.

When I grow rich,
Say the bells at Shoreditch.

Pray, when will that be?
Say the bells of Stepney.

I am sure I don't know,
Says the great bell at Bow.

Here comes a candle to light you to bed,
And here comes a chopper to chop off your head.

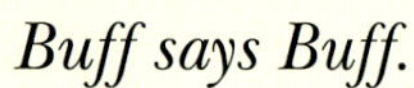

Buff says Buff.

BUFF says Buff to all his men,
And I say Buff to you again;
Buff neither laughs nor smiles,
But carries his face
With a very good grace,
And passes the stick to the very next place!

Hark, hark! the Dogs do Bark!

HARK, hark!
The dogs do bark,
The beggars are coming to town
  Some in rags,
  Some in jags,
And some in velvet gowns.

A Swarm of Bees in May.

SWARM of Bees in May
Is worth a load of hay;
A swarm of bees in June
Is worth a silver spoon;
A swarm of bees in July
Is not worth a fly.

For Want of a Nail.

FOR want of a nail, the shoe was lost,
For want of the shoe, the horse was lost,
For want of the horse, the rider was lost,
For want of the rider, the battle was lost,
For want of the battle, the kingdom was lost,
And all from the want of a horseshoe nail !

Fiddle-de-dee.

FIDDLE-DE-DEE, fiddle-de-dee,
The fly shall marry the humble-bee.
They went to the church, and married was she,
The fly has married the humble-bee.

Elizabeth, Elspeth.

ELIZABETH, Elspeth, Betsy, and Bess,
They all went together to seek a bird's nest.
They found a bird's nest with five eggs in,
They all took one, and left four in.

Little Miss Muffet.

LITTLE Miss Muffet
  Sat on a tuffet,
Eating of curds and whey;
  There came a spider,
  And sat down beside her,
And frightened Miss Muffet away.

My Lady Wind, my Lady Wind.

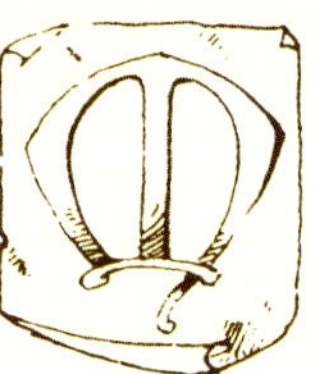

y Lady Wind, my Lady wind,
  Went round about the house to find
    A chink to get her foot in.
She tried the key-hole in the door,
She tried the crevice in the floor,
And drove the chimney soot in.

And then one night when it was dark,
She blew up such a tiny spark,
  That all the house was bothered:
From it she raised up such a flame,
As flamed away to Belting Lane,
  And White Cross folks were smothered.

And thus when once, my little dears,
A whisper reaches itching ears,
  The same will come, you'll find:
Take my advice, restrain the tongue,
Remember what old Nurse has sung
  Of busy Lady Wind!

Little Miss Muffet.

Jacky, come, give Me thy Fiddle.

JACKY, come, give me thy fiddle,
   If ever thou mean to thrive;
Nay; I'll not give my fiddle
   To any man alive.

If I should give my fiddle,
   They'll think that I'm gone mad;
For many a joyful day
   My fiddle and I have had.

A Little Old Old Man.

A LITTLE old man of Derby,
How do you think he served me?
He took away my bread and cheese,
And that is how he served me.

The Sow came in with the Saddle.

THE SOW came in with the saddle,
The little Pig rocked the cradle,
The Dish jumped on the table,
To see the Pot swallow the Ladle.
The Spit that stood behind the door
Threw the Pudding-stick on the floor.
"Odsplut! "said the Gridiron, "can't you agree?
I'm the head constable,— bring them to me."

A Sunshiny Shower.

A SUNSHINY Shower
Won't last half an hour.

Some Little Mice Sat.

SOME little mice sat in a barn to spin;
Pussy came by, and popped her head in;
"Shall I come in, and cut your threads off?"
"Oh! no, kind sir, you could snap our heads off."

I had a Little Nut-tree.

I HAD a little nut-tree; nothing would it bear
But a silver nutmeg and a golden pear;
The King of Spain's daughter came to visit me
And all because of my little nut-tree.
I skipped over water, I danced over sea,
And all the birds in the air couldn't catch me.

If Ifs and Ands.

IF ifs and ands
Were pots and pans,
There would be no need for tinkers!

Come when You're Called.

COME when you're called,
Do what you're bid,
Shut the door after you,
Never be chid.

As I was Going Up Pippen Hill.

As I was going up Pippen Hill—,
Pippen Hill was dirty,—,
There I met a pretty miss,
And she dropped me a curtsey.

Little miss, pretty miss,
Blessings light upon you!
If I had half-a-crown a day,
I'd spend it all upon you.

HE fox and his wife they had a great strife,
They never ate mustard in all their whole life;
They ate their meat without fork or knife,
    And loved to be picking a bone, e-ho!

The fox jumped up on a moonlight night;
The stars they were shining, and all things bright;
"O ho!" said the fox, "it's a very fine night
    For me to go through the town, e-ho!"

The fox, when he came to yonder stile,
He lifted his lugs and he listened a while!
"O ho!" said the fox, "it's but a short mile
    From this unto yonder wee town, e-ho!"

The fox, when he came to the farmer's gate,
Who should he see but the farmer's drake;
"I love you well for your master's sake,
    And long to be picking your bone, e-ho!"

The Grey Goose She Ran.

The grey goose

she ran

round the hay-stack,

"Oho!" said the fox,

"you are very fat;

You'll grease my beard,

and ride on my back

From this

unto yonder wee town,

e-ho!"

Old Gammer Hipple-hopple

hopped out of bed,

She opened the casement,

and popped out her head:

"Oh husband! Oh husband!

the grey goose is dead

And the fox has gone

through the town O!"

Then the old man got up in his red cap,
And swore he would catch the fox in a trap;
But the fox was too cunning, and gave him the slip
    And ran through the town, the town, O!

When he got to the top of the hill,
He blew his trumpet both loud and shrill,
For joy that he was safe
    Through the town, O!

When the fox came back to his den,
He had young ones both nine and ten,
"You're welcome home, daddy, you may go again,
If you bring us such nice meat
    From the town, O!"

As I was Going up the Hill.

 As I was going up the hill,
  I met with Jack the piper,
 And all the tune that he could play
  was, "Tie up your petticoats tighter."

 I tied them once, I tied them twice,
  I tied them three times over;
 And all the song that he could sing
  Was, "Carry me safe to Dover."

Bryan O'Lin

BRYAN O'LIN, and his wife, and wife's mother,
They all went over the bridge together;
The bridge was broken, and they all fell in—
"The deuce go with all!" quoth Bryan O'Lin.

Buz, quoth the Blue Fly.

BUZ, quoth the blue fly,
Hum, quoth the bee;
Buz and hum, they Cry,
And so do we.
In his ear, in his nose,
Thus, do you see?
He ate the dormouse,
Else it was he.

He that would Thrive.

HE that would thrive
Must rise at five;
He that hath thriven
May lie till seven;
And he that by the plough would thrive,
Himself must either hold or drive.

I Doubt, I Doubt.

I DOUBT, I doubt my fire's all out,
My little dame is not at home?
I'll saddle my cock, and bridle my hen,
And fetch my little dame home again!

Doctor Faustus.

DOCTOR FAUSTUS was a good man
He whipped his scholars now and then;
When he whipped them, he made them dance
Out of Scotland into France,
Out of France into Spain,
And then he whipped them back again!

Father Short.

FATHER SHORT came down the lane,
Oh, I'm obliged to hammer and smite
From four in the morning till eight at night,
For a bad master, and a worse dame.

I had a Little Husband.

I HAD a little husband,
    No bigger than my thumb;
I put him in a pint pot,
    And there I bid him drum.

I bought a little horse,
    That galloped up and down;
I bridled him, and saddled him,
    And sent him out of town.

I gave him some garters,
    To garter up his nose,
And a little handkerchief
    To wipe his pretty nose.

Higgledy, Piggledy, here We Lie.

HIGGLEDY, piggledy,
    Here we lie,
Picked and plucked,
    And put in a pie.
My first is snapping, snarling, growling,
My second's industrious, romping, and prowling.
    Higgledy, piggledy,
    Here we lie,
Picked and plucked,
    And put in a pie.
            (*Currants.*)

Here We Come Gathering.

HERE we come gathering
nuts and may,
Nuts and may, nuts and may,
Here we come gathering
nuts and may,
On a cold and frosty morning.

As I was going to St. Ives

AS I was going to St. Ives,
I met a man with seven wives,
Every wife had seven sacks,
Every sack had seven cats,
Every cat had seven kits—
Kits, cats, sacks, and wives,
How many were there going to St. Ives?

(*One.*)

Merry are the Bells.

MERRY are the bells, and merry would they ring,
Merry was myself, and merry could I sing;
With a merry ding-dong, happy, gay, and free,
And a merry sing-song, happy let us be!

Waddle goes your gait, and hollow are your hose,
Noddle goes your pate, and purple is your nose;
Merry is your sing-song, happy, gay, and free,
With a merry ding-dong, happy let us be!

Merry have we met, and merry have we been,
Merry let us part, and merry meet again;
With our merry sing-song, happy, gay, and free,
And a merry ding-dong, happy let us be!

A FROG he would a-wooing go,
    Sing heigho, says Rowley,
Whether his mother would let him or no;
With a rowley, powley, gammon. and spinach,
    Heigho, says Anthony Rowley,

So off he marches with his opera hat,
    Heigho, says Rowley,
And on the way he met with a rat,
    With a rowley, powley etc.

And when they came to Mouse's Hall,
    Heigho, says Rowley,
They gave a loud knock, and they gave a loud call,
    With a rowley, powley, etc.

"Pray, Mrs. Mouse, are you within?"
 Heigho, says Rowley;
"Yes, kind sir, I am sitting to spin,"
 With a rowley, powley, etc.

"Pray, Mrs. Mouse, will you give us some beer?"
 Heigho, says Rowley;
"For froggy and I are fond of good cheer,"
 With a rowley, powley, etc.

Now while they all were a merry-making,
 Heigho, says Rowley,
The cat and her kittens came tumbling in,
 With a rowley, powley, etc.

The cat she seized the rat by the crown,
　　Heigho, says Rowley;
The kittens they pulled the little mouse down,
　　With a rowley, powley, etc.

This put poor frog in a terrible fright,
　　Heigho, says Rowley,
So he took up his hat and wished them good-night,
　　With a rowley, powley, etc.

But as Froggy was crossing over a brook,
    Heigho, says Rowley,
A lily-white duck came and gobbled him up,
    With a rowley, powley, etc.

So there was an end of one, two, and three,
    Heigho, says Rowley,
The rat, the mouse, and the little Frog-ee!
with a rowley, powley, gammon, and spinach,
    Heigho, says Anthony Rowley.

As Round as an Apple.

As round as an apple, as deep as a cup,
And all the king's horses can't pull it up.
          (*A Well.*)

If all the seas were one sea.

If All the Seas were One Sea.

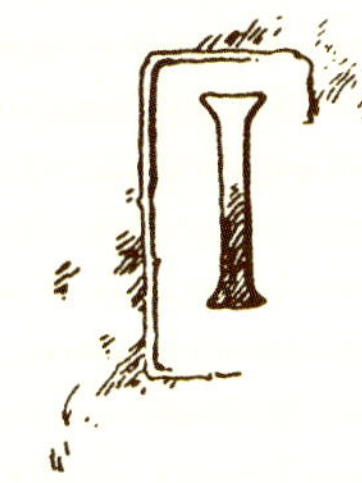

I
F all the seas were one sea,
What a *great* sea that would be!
And if all the trees were one tree,
What a *great* tree that would be!
And if all the axes were one axe,
What a *great* axe that would be !

And if all the men were one man,
What a *great* man he would be!
And if the *great* man took the *great* axe,
And cut down the *great* tree,
And let it fall into the *great* sea,
What a splish splash *that* would be!

The Dove Says, "Coo, coo."

THE dove says, "Coo, coo, what shall I do"?
I can scarce maintain two."
"Pooh! pooh! "Says the wren; "I have got ten,
And I keep them all like gentlemen."

A Little Pig Found

A LITTLE Pig found a fifty-dollar note,
And purchased a hat and a very fine coat,
With trousers, and stockings, and shoes;
Cravat, and shirt-collar, and gold-headed cane;
Then, proud as could be, did he march up the lane;
Says he, "I shall hear all the news."

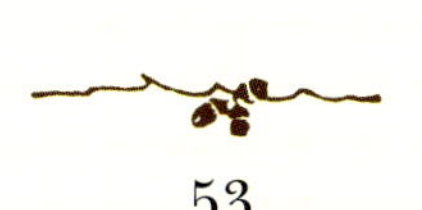

Up Hill and Down Dale.

Up hill and down dale;
Butter is made in every vale;
And if that Nancy Cook
Is a good girl,
She shall have a spouse,
And make butter anon,
Before her old grandmother
Grows a young man.

How Many Miles to Babylon?

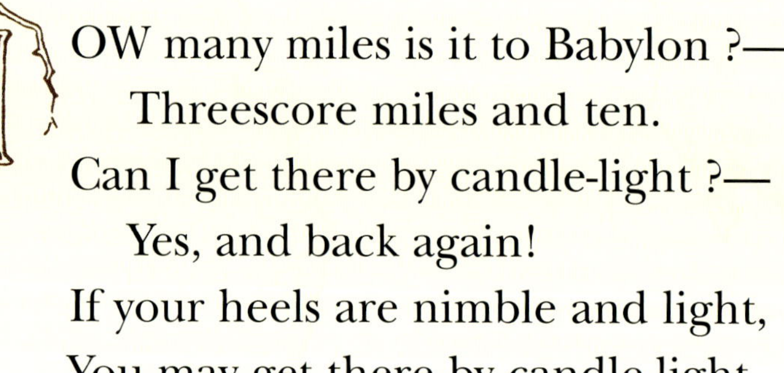

OW many miles is it to Babylon?—
Threescore miles and ten.
Can I get there by candle-light?—
Yes, and back again!
If your heels are nimble and light,
You may get there by candle-light.

There Was a Little Green House.

There was a Little Green House,
And in the little green house
There was a little brown house,
And in the little brown house
There was a little yellow house,
And in the little yellow house
There was a little white house,
And in the little white house
There was a little heart.

(*A walnut.*)

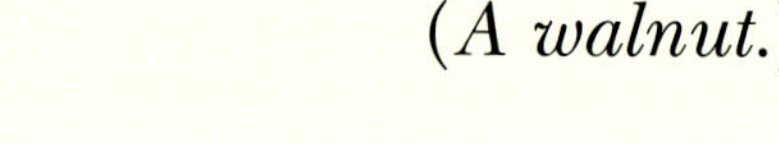

See-saw, Margery Daw.

SEE-SAW Margery Daw,
Jenny shall have a new master:
She shall have but a penny a day,
Because she can't work any faster.

Whistle, Daughter, Whistle.

WHISTLE, daughter, whistle, daughter dear.
I cannot whistle, mammy, I cannot whistle clear.
Whistle, daughter, whistle, whistle for a pound.
I cannot whistle, mammy, I cannot make a sound.

Bat, Bat, Come under My Hat.

BAT, bat,
Come under my hat,
And I'll give you a slice of bacon;
And when I bake
I'll give you a cake,
If I am not mistaken.

Monday's Child.

MONDAY'S child is fair of face,
Tuesday's child is full of grace,
Wednesday's child is full of woe,
Thursday's child has far to go,
Friday's child is loving and giving,
Saturday's child works hard for its living;
And a child that is born on Christmas Day
Is fair, and wise, and good, and gay.

If All the World.

IF all the world was apple-pie,
And all the sea was ink,
And all the trees were bread and cheese,
What should we have for drink?

Multiplication is Vexation.

MULTIPLICATION is vexation,
Division is just as bad;
The rule of Three perplexes me,
And Practice drives me mad.

Multiplication is Vexation.

Humpty Dumpty.

HUMPTY DUMPTY sat on a wall,
Humpty Dumpty had a great fall;
Threescore men and threescore more
Cannot place Humpty Dumpty as he was before.

Hot Cross Buns!

HOT-cross buns!
Hot-cross buns!
One a penny, two a penny,
Hot-cross buns!

Hot-cross buns!
Hot-cross buns!
If ye have no daughters,
Give them to your sons.

Did You See My Wife?

DID you see my wife, did you see, did you see,
　　Did you see my wife looking for me?
She wears a straw bonnet, with white ribbons on it,
　　And dimity petticoats over her knee.

Birds of a Feather.

BIRDS of a feather flock together,
　　And so will pigs and swine;
Rats and mice will have their choice,
　　And so will I have mine.

Wooley Foster has Gone to Sea.

WOOLEY FOSTER has gone to sea,
With silver buckles at his knee;
When he comes back he'll marry me,
　　Bonny Wooley Foster

Wooley Foster has a cow,
Black and white about the mow;
Open the gates and let her through,
　　Wooley Foster's ain cow!

Wooley Foster has a hen,
Cockle button, cockle ben,
She lays eggs for gentlemen,
　　But none for Wooley Foster.

A Dillar, a Dollar.

A DILLAR, a dollar,
A ten o'clock scholar,
What makes you come so soon?
You used to come at ten o'clock,
And now you come at noon.

Awa', Birds, Away!

AWA', birds, away!
Take a little, leave a little,
And do not come again;
For if you do,
I will shoot you through,
And there is an end of you.

Charley, Charley!

CHARLEY, Charley, stole the barley
Out of the baker's shop;
The baker came out, and gave him a clout,
And made poor Charley hop.

Jeannie Come Tie my Bonnie Cravat.

JEANNIE, come tie my,
Jeannie, come tie my,
Jeannie, come tie my bonnie cravat;
I've tied it behind,
I've tied it before,
And I've tied it so often, I'll tie it no more.

"What makes you come so soon?"

TOM, Tom, the piper's son.

TOM, Tom the piper's son,
He learned to play when he was young;
But all the tunes that he could play
Was "Over the hills and far away,"
Over the hills, and a great way off,
And the wind will blow my top-knot off.

NOW, Tom with his pipe made such a noise,
That he pleased both the girls and boys,
And they stopped to hear him play,
"Over the hills and far away."

Tom with his pipe did play with such skill
That those who heard him could never keep still:
Whenever they heard they began for to dance,—
Even pigs on their hind legs
would after him prance.

As Dolly was milking her cow one day,
Tom took out his pipe and began for to play;
So Doll and the cow danced "the Cheshire round,"
Till the pail was broke,
and the milk ran on the ground.

He met old Dame Trot with a basket of eggs,
He used his pipe and she used her legs;
She danced about till the eggs were all broke,
She began for to fret, but he laughed at the joke.

He saw a cross fellow was beating an ass,
Heavy laden with pots, pans, dishes, and glass;
He took out his pipe and played them a tune,
And the jackass's load was lightened full soon.

As I Was Going Along.

As I was going along, long, long,
A-singing a comical song, song, song,
The lane that I went was so long, long, long,
And the song that I sung was as long, long, long,
And so I went singing along.

I Would if I Could.

I WOULD if I could,
If I couldn't how could I?
I couldn't without I could, could I?
Could you, without you could, could ye?
Could ye, could ye?
Could you, without you could, could ye?

Lavender Blue and Rosemary Green.

LAVENDER blue and Rosemary green,
When I am king you shall be queen;
Call up my maids at four of the clock,
Some to the wheel, and some to the rock,
Some to make hay, and some to thresh corn,
And you and I will keep the bed warm.

I Went to the Wood.

I WENT to the wood and got it;
I sat me down and looked at it;
The more I looked at it the less I liked it,
And I brought it home because I couldn't help it.

(*A thorn.*)

l Had a Little Cow.

    I HAD a little cow;
        Hey-diddle, ho-diddle !
    I had a little cow, and it had a little calf;
        Hey-diddle, ho-diddle;
           and there's my song half.

    I had a little cow;
        Hey-diddle, ho-diddle !
    I had a little cow, and I drove it to the stall;
        Hey-diddle, ho-diddle;
           and there's my song all !

Little Cock Robin.

LITTLE Cock Robin peeped out of his cabin
To see the cold winter come in.
Tit for tat, what matter for that ?—
He'll hide his head under his wing !

Mary had a Little Lamb

MARY had a little lamb,
  Its fleece was white as snow;
  And everywhere that Mary went,
  The lamb was sure to go.

He followed her to school one day;
  That was against the rule;
  It made the children laugh and play
  To see a lamb at school.

And so the teacher turned him out,
  But still he lingered near,
  And waited patiently about
  Till Mary did appear.

Mary had a little lamb.

Then he ran to her, and laid
 His head upon her arm,
As if he said, "I'm not afraid—
 You'll keep me from all harm."

"What makes the lamb love Mary so?
 The eager children cry.
"Oh, Mary loves the lamb, you know,"
 The teacher did reply.

And you each gentle animal
 In confidence may bind,
And make them follow at your will,
 If you are only kind.

Here am I.

HERE am I,
Little jumping Joan.
When nobody's with me,
I'm always alone.

Hurly, Burly.

HURLY, burly, trumpet trase,
The cow was in the market-place.
Some goes far, and some goes near,
But where shall this poor henchman steer?

I Went up One Pair of Stairs.

1. I WENT UP one pair of stairs.
2. Just like me.
1. I went up two pair of stairs.
2. Just like me.
1. I went into a room.
2. Just like me.
1. I looked out of a window.
2. Just like me.
1. And there I saw a monkey.
2. Just like me.

Elsie Marley.

ELSIE MARLEY has grown so fine
She won't get up to feed the swine;
She lies in bed till half-past nine—
Ay! truly she doth take her time.

Poor Dog Bright.

> POOR Dog Bright
> Ran off with all his might,
> Because the cat was after him—
> Poor Dog Bright !
>
> Poor Cat Fright
> Ran off with all her might,
> Because the dog was after her—
> Poor Cat Fright !

Johnny Shall Have A New Bonnet.

JOHNNY shall have a new bonnet,
    And Johnny shall go to the fair,
And Johnny shall have a blue ribbon
    To tie up his bonny brown hair.

And why may not I love Johnny?
    And why may not Johnny love me?
And why may not I love Johnny
    As well as another body?

 And here's a leg for a stocking,
    And here's a leg, for a shoe;
And he has a kiss for his daddy,
    And two for his mammy, I trow.

And why may not I love Johnny?
    And why may not Johnny love me?
And why may not I love Johnny
As well as another body?

A Cat Came Fiddling Out of a Barn.

CAT came fiddling out of a barn,
With a pair of bag-pipes under her arm;
She could sing nothing but fiddle-de-dee,
The mouse has married the humble-bee;
Pipe, cat—dance, mouse—
We'll have a wedding at our good house.

*I'll Sing you a Song,
though Not Very Long.*

I'LL sing you a song,
Though not very long,
Yet I think it's
as pretty as any;
Put your hand
in your purse,
You'll never be worse,
And give the
poor singer
a penny.

Pussy-cat, Pussycat.

PUSSY-CAT
Pussy-cat,
where have you been?

"I've been
up to London
to look at the Queen."

Pussy-cat, pussy-cat,
what did you there?
"I frightened
a little mouse
under the chair."

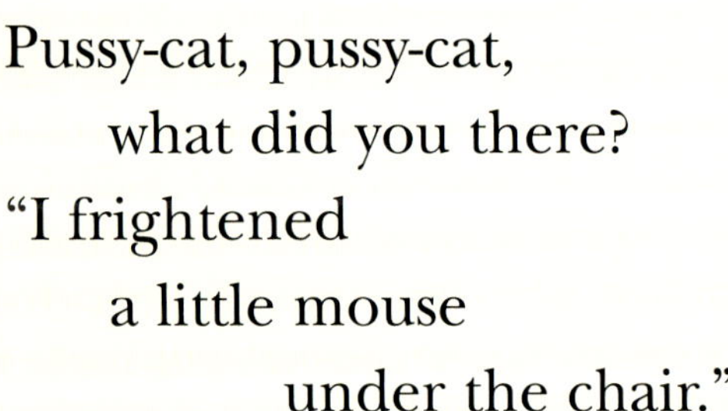

I Had a Little Hen.

I Had a Little Hen.

I HAD a little hen, the prettiest ever seen;
She washed me the dishes, and kept the house clean;
She went to the mill to fetch me some flour,
She brought it home in less than an hour;
She baked me my bread, she brewed me my ale,
She sat by the fire and told many a fine tale.

Marble Walls.

> IN marble walls as white as milk,
> Lined with a skin as soft as silk,
> Within a fountain crystal clear,
> A golden apple doth appear.
> No doors there are to this stronghold,
> Yet thieves break in and steal the gold.
>
> *(An egg.)*

A man of Words.

> A MAN of words and not of deeds
> Is like a garden full of weeds;
> For when the weeds begin to grow,
> Then doth the garden overflow.

Hey Diddle, Dinketty.

HEY diddle, dinketty, pompetty, pet,
The merchants of London they wear scarlet;
Silk in the collar, and gold in the hem,
So merrily march the merchantmen.

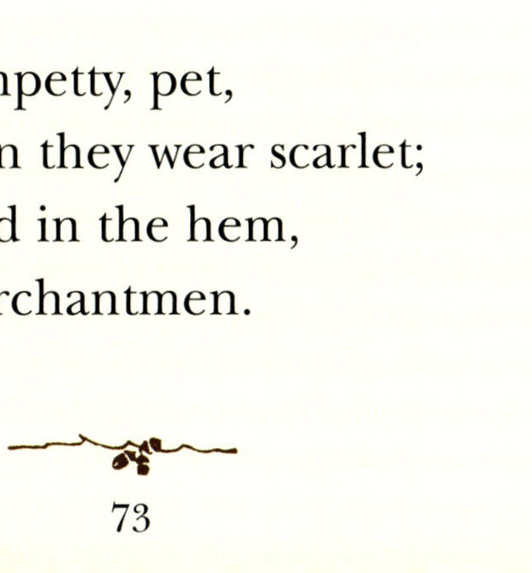

I Saw Three Ships

I SAW three ships come sailing by,
    Come sailing by, come sailing by;
I saw three ships come sailing by,
    New Year's Day in the morning.

And what do you think was in them then?
    Was in them then, was in them then?
And what do you think was in them then?
    New Year's Day in the morning.

Three pretty girls were in them then,
    Were in them then, were in them then,
Three pretty girls were in them then,
    New Year's Day in the morning.

One could whistle, and another could sing,
    And the other could play on the violin—
Such joy was there at my wedding,
    New Year's Day in the morning.

As I Went Through the Garden Gap.

    As I went through the garden gap!
    Who should I meet but Dick Red-cap!
    A stick in his hand, a stone in his throat.
    If you'll tell me this riddle, I'll give you a groat.
                    (*A cherry.*)

I SAW Three Ships!

Jack and Jill.

Jack and Jill went up the hill,
To fetch a pail of water;
Jack fell down, and broke his crown,
And Jill came tumbling after.

Dame, Get Up, and Bake Your Pies.

DAME, get up and bake your pies,
Bake your pies, bake your pies,
Dame, get up and bake your pies,
On Christmas-day in the morning

Dame, what makes your maidens lie,
Maidens lie, maidens lie;
Dame, what makes your maidens lie,
On Christmas-day in the morning?

Dame, what makes your ducks to die,
Ducks to die, ducks to die;
Dame, what makes your ducks to die,
On Christmas-day in the morning?

Their wings are cut, and they cannot fly,
Cannot fly, cannot fly;
Their wings are cut, and they cannot fly,
On Christmas-day in the morning.

Jack and Jill.

As I Walked by Myself.

AS I walked by myself,
And talked to myself,
Myself said unto me,
Look to thyself, Take care of thyself,
For nobody cares for thee.
I answered myself,
And said to myself
In the self-same repartee,
Look to thyself, Or not look to thyself,
The self-same thing will be.

As I was Going.

As I was going o'er London Bridge,
I met a cart full of fingers and thumbs!
(*Gloves.*)

Great A, Little a.

> GREAT A, little a,
> Bouncing B!
> The cat's in the cupboard,
> And she can't see.

Jack Sprat.

> JACK SPRAT could eat no fat,
>   His wife could eat no lean;
> Betwixt them both, they cleared the plate,
>   And licked the platter clean.

As I Went to Bonner.

> As I went to Bonner,
>   I met a pig
>   Without a wig,
> Upon my word and honour.

A Riddle, a Riddle.

A RIDDLE, a riddle, as I suppose,
A hundred eyes, and never a nose. (*A cinder- sifter.*)

Is John Smith Within?

> Is John Smith within?
> Yes, that he is.
> Can he set a shoe ?—
> Ay, marry, two;
> Here a nail, and there a nail,
> Tick, tack, too.

The Old Woman Who Rode
on a Broom.

THERE was an old woman who rode on a broom,
    With a high gee ho, gee humble;
And she took her old cat behind for a groom,
    With a bimble, bamble, bumble.

They travelled along till they came to the sky,
    With a high gee ho, gee humble;
But the journey so long made them very hungry,
    With a bimble, bamble, bumble.

Says Tom, "I can find nothing here to eat,
    with a high gee ho, gee humble;
So let us go back again, I entreat,
    with a bimble, bamble, bumble."

The old woman would not go back so soon,
    with a high gee ho, gee humble;
For she wanted to visit the man in the moon,
    with a bimble, bamble, bumble.

Says Tom, "I'll go back myself to our house,
    With a high gee ho, gee humble;
For there I can catch a good rat or a mouse,
    with a bimble, bamble, bumble."

"But," says the old woman, "how will you go?
    With a high gee ho, gee humble;
You shan't have my nag, I protest and vow,
    With a bimble, bamble, bumble."

"No, no," says Tom, "I've a plan of my own,
    With a high gee ho, gee humble;"
So he slid down the rainbow,
    With a bimble, bamble, bumble.

So now, if you happen to visit the sky,
    With a high gee ho, gee humble,
And want to come back, you Tom's method may try,
    with a bimble, bamble, bumble.

Feeding the Chicks.

Cock a Doodle Doo!

COCK a doodle doo!
My dame has lost her shoe;
My master's lost his fiddling-stick,
And don't know what to do.

Cock a doodle doo!
What is my dame to do?
Till master finds his fiddling-stick,
She'll dance without her shoe.

Cock a doodle doo !
My dame has lost her shoe,
And master's found his fiddling-stick,
Sing doodle doodle doo!

Cock a doodle doo,
My dame will dance with you,
While master fiddles his fiddling-stick,
For dame and doodle doo.

Cock a doodle doo!
Dame has lost her shoe;
Gone to bed and scratched her head,
And can't tell what to do.

Cock Crows in the Morn.

COCK crows in the morn,
  To tell us to rise,
And he who lies late
  will never be wise:

For early to bed,
  And early to rise,
Is the way to be healthy
  And wealthy and wise.

Little Bob Robin.

LITTLE Bob Robin, where do you live?
Up in yon wood, sir, on a hazel twig.

The Old Man Who Lived in a Wood.

THERE was an old man who lived in a wood,
    As you may plainly see;
He said he could do as much work in a day
    As his wife could do in three.
"With all my heart," the old woman said;
    "If that you will allow,
To-morrow you'll stay at home in my stead,
    And I'll go drive the plough."

"But you must milk the Tidy cow,
    For fear that she go dry;
And you must feed the little pigs
    That are within the sty;
And you must mind the speckled hen,
    For fear she lay away;
And you must reel the spool of yarn
    That I spun yesterday."

High! Tidy l ho! Tidy! high!
    Tidy, do stand still!
If ever I milk you, Tidy, again,
    'Twill be sore against my will."
He went to feed the little pigs,
    That were within the sty;
He hit his head against the beam,
    And he made the blood to fly.

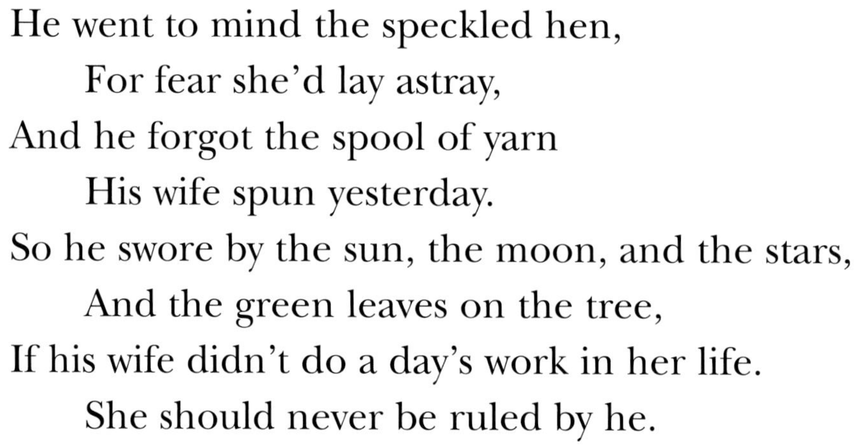

He went to mind the speckled hen,
For fear she'd lay astray,
And he forgot the spool of yarn
His wife spun yesterday.
So he swore by the sun, the moon, and the stars,
And the green leaves on the tree,
If his wife didn't do a day's work in her life.
She should never be ruled by he.

Dance, Little Baby.

DANCE, little baby, dance up high,
Never mind, baby, mother is by;
Crow and caper, caper and crow,
There, little baby, there you go;

Up to the ceiling, down to the ground,
Backwards and forwards, round and round;
Dance, little baby, and mother will sing,
with the merry coral, ding, ding, ding!

Flour of England.

FLOUR of England, fruit of Spain,
Met together in a shower of rain;
Put in a bag tied round with a string,
If you'll tell me this riddle, I'll give you a ring.
(*A plum pudding*)

R UB- A-DUB-DUB,
  Three men in a tub,
And who who you think they be?
  The butcher, the baker,
  The candlestick-maker;
    Turn 'em out, knaves all three!

Moss Was a Little Man.

Moss was a little man, and a little mare did buy;
For kicking and for sprawling, none her could come nigh;
She could trot, she could amble,
       and could canter here and there,
But one night she strayed away—so Moss lost his mare.

Moss got up next morning to catch her fast asleep,
And round about the frosty fields so nimbly he did creep.
Dead in a ditch he found her,
       and glad to find her there;
So I'll tell you by-and-by how Moss caught his mare.

"Rise! stupid, rise!" he thus to her did say;
"Arise, you beast, you drowsy beast, get up without delay,
For I must ride you to the town,
       so don't lie sleeping there;
He put the halter round her neck— so Moss caught his mare.

Old Mistress McShuttle.

OLD Mistress McShuttle
Lived in a coal-scuttle,
Along with her dog and her cat:
What they ate I can't tell,
But 'tis known very well
That none of the party were fat.

LITTLE TOMMY Tittlemouse
Lived in a little house;
He caught fishes
In other men's ditches.

Up at Piccadilly, Oh!

UP at Piccadilly, oh !
   The coachman takes his stand,
And when he meets a pretty girl,
   He takes her by the hand.
Whip away for ever, oh!
   Drive away so clever, oh!
All the way to Bristol, oh!
   He drives her four-in-hand.

Joey Was A bad man.

JOEY was a bad man, Joey was a thief;
Joey came to my house and stole a piece of beef;

I went to Joey's house, Joey was not at home;
Joey came to my house and stole a marrow-bone.

I went to Joey's house, Joey was asleep,
I took the marrow-bone, and beat about his feet.

There was a Fat Man of Bombay.

THERE was a fat man of Bombay,
Who was smoking one sunshiny day,
When a bird, called a snipe,
Flew away with his pipe,
Which vexed the fat man of Bombay.

Sing a Song of Sixpence.

SING a song of sixpence,
A pocket full of rye;
Four and twenty blackbirds
Baked in a pie;

When the pie was opened,
The birds began to sing;
Was not that a dainty dish
To set before the king?

The king was in the parlour,
Counting out his money;
The queen was in the kitchen,
Eating bread and honey;

The maid was in the garden,
Hanging out the clothes;
There came a little blackbird,
And snipped off her nose.

The Queen of Hearts.

THE queen of hearts
    She made some tarts,
All on a summer's day;
The knave of hearts
    He stole those tarts,
And with them ran away.

The king of hearts
    Called for those tarts,
And beat the knave full sore;
The knave of hearts
    Brought back those tarts,
And said he'd ne'er steal more.

Sing a Song of Sixpence

SING a song of sixpence,
    A pocket full of rye;
        Four-and-twenty blackbirds
        Baked in a pie.

Jack and Jill.

JACK AND JILL
 went up the hill
To fetch a pail of water;
Jack fell down
 and broke his crown,
And Jill came tumbling after.

Then up Jack got
 and home did trot
As fast as he could caper;
Dame Gill did the job
 to plaster his head
With vinegar and brown paper.

Where Are You Going, My Pretty Maid?

"WHERE are you going, my pretty maid?"
"I'm going a-milking, sir," she said.

"May I go with you, my pretty maid?"
"You're kindly welcome, sir," she said.

"What is your father, my pretty maid?"
"My father's a farmer, sir," she said.

"What is your fortune, my pretty maid?"
"My face is my fortune, sir," she said.

"Then I can't marry you, my pretty maid!"
"Nobody asked you, sir!" she said.

Here We Go Up, Up, Up.

HERE we go up, up, up,
  And here we go down, down, downy,
And here we go backwards and forwards,
  And here we go round, round, roundy.

Oh, Dear What Can the Matter Be?

OH, dear! what can the matter be?
Two old women got up an apple-tree;
One came down,
And the other stayed till Saturday.

For Every Evil Under the Sun.

FOR every evil under the sun,
There is a remedy, or there is none.
If there be one, try and find it,
If there be none, never mind it.

PLEASE to remember
The Fifth of November,
Gunpowder, treason, and plot;
I know no reason
Why gunpowder treason
Should ever be forgot.

See, Saw, Sacradown.

> SEE, saw, sacradown,
> Which is the way to London town?
> One foot up, the other foot down,
> And that is the way to London town.

Little Boy Blue.

> LITTLE Boy Blue, come blow up your horn,
> The sheep's in the meadow, the cow's in the corn;
>
> Where's the little boy that tends the sheep?
> He's under the haycock, fast asleep.
>
> Go wake him, go wake him. Oh! no, not I;
> For if I awake him, he'll certainly cry.

Once I Saw a little Bird.

> ONCE I saw a little bird
>   Come hop, hop, hop;
> So I cried, "Little bird,
>   Will you stop, stop, stop?"
> And was going to the window
>   To say, "How do you do?"
> But he shook his little tail,
>   And far away he flew.
>
> SEE, see! what shall I see?
> A horse's head where his tail should be!

*The Marriage of Cock Robin
and Jenny Wren.*

IT was on a merry time,
　　When Jenny Wren was young,
So neatly as she danced,
　　And so sweetly as she sung,—

Robin Redbreast lost his heart:
　　He was a gallant bird;
He doffed his hat to Jenny,
　　And thus to her he said:

"My dearest Jenny Wren,
　　If you will but be mine,
You shall dine on cherry-pie,
　　And drink nice currant-wine.

"I'll dress you like a Goldfinch,
　　Or like a Peacock gay;
So if you'll have me, Jenny,
　　Let us appoint the day."

Jenny blushed behind her fan,
    And thus declared her mind:
"Then let it be to-morrow, Bob;
    I take your offer kind.

"Cherry-pie is very good;
    So is currant-wine;
But I will wear my brown gown,
    And never dress too fine."

Robin rose up early,
    At the break of day;
He flew to Jenny Wren's house,
    To sing a roundelay.

He met the Cock and Hen,
    And bade the Cock declare,
This was his wedding-day
    With Jenny wren the fair.

The Cock then blew his horn,
    To let the neighbours know
This was Robin's wedding-day,
    And they might see the show.

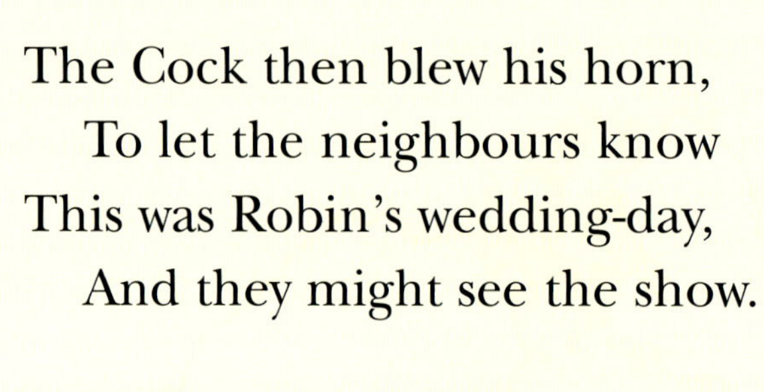

And first came Parson Rook,
    With his spectacles and band;
And one of Mother Hubbard's books
    He held within his hand.

Then followed him the Lark,
    For he could sweetly sing;
And he was to be clerk
    At Cock Robin's wedding.

He sang of Robin's love
    For little Jenny Wren;
And when he came unto the end,
    Then he began again.

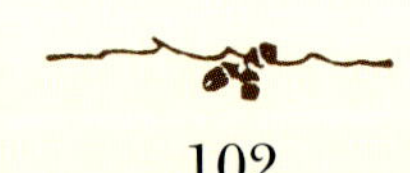

The Goldfinch came on next,
   To give away the bride;
The Linnet, being bridesmaid,
   Walked by Jenny's side.

And as she was a walking,
   Said, "Upon my word,
I think that your Cock Robin
   Is a very pretty bird."

The Blackbird and the Thrush,
   And charming Nightingale;
whose sweet "jug" sweetly echoes
   Through every grove and dale;

The Sparrow and Tomtit,
   And many more were there;
All came to see the wedding
   Of Jenny Wren the fair.

The Marriage.

The Bullfinch walked by Robin,
   And thus to him did say:
"Pray, mark, friend Robin Redbreast,
   That Goldfinch dressed so gay;

"What though her gay apparel
   Becomes her very well;
Yet Jenny's modest dress and look
   Must bear away the bell!"

Then came the bride and bridegroom;
   Quite plainly was she dressed;
And blushed so much, her cheeks were
   As red as Robin's breast.

But Robin cheered her up;
   "My pretty Jen," said he,
"We're going to be married,
   And happy we shall be."

"Oh, then," says Parson Rook,
   "Who gives this maid away?"
"I do," says the Goldfinch,
   "And her fortune I will pay;

"Here's a bag of grain of many sorts,
   And other things beside;
Now happy be the bridegroom,
   And happy be the bride!"

"And will you have her, Robin
    To be your wedded wife?"
"Yes, I will," says Robin,
    "And love her all my life."

"And you will have him, Jenny,
    Your husband now to be?"
"Yes, I will," says Jenny,
    "And love him heartily."

Then on her finger fair,
    Cock Robin put the ring;
"You're married now," says Parson Rook;
    while the Lark aloud did sing:

"Happy be the bridegroom,
    And happy be the bride!
And may not man, nor bird, nor beast,
    This happy pair divide."

The birds were asked to dine;
    Not Jenny's friends alone,
But every pretty songster
    That had Cock Robin known.

They had a cherry-pie,
    Besides some currant-wine,
And every guest brought something,
    That sumptuous they might dine.

The Wedding Breakfast.

Now they all sat or stood,
　　To eat and to drink;
And every one said what
　　He happened to think.

They each took a bumper,
　　And drank to the pair;
Cock Robin the bridegroom,
　　And Jenny Wren the fair.

The dinner things removed,
　　They all began to sing;
And soon they made the place
　　Near a mile around to ring.

The concert it was fine;
    And every bird tried
Who best should sing for Robin,
    And Jenny Wren the bride,

When in came the Cuckoo,
    And made a great rout;
He caught hold of Jenny,
    And pulled her about.

Cock Robin was angry,
    And so was the Sparrow,
Who fetched in a hurry
    His bow and his arrow.

His aim then he took,
    But he took it not right;
His skill was not good,
    Or he shot in a fright;

For the Cuckoo he missed,
    But Cock Robin he killed!—
And all the birds mourned
    That his blood was so spilled.

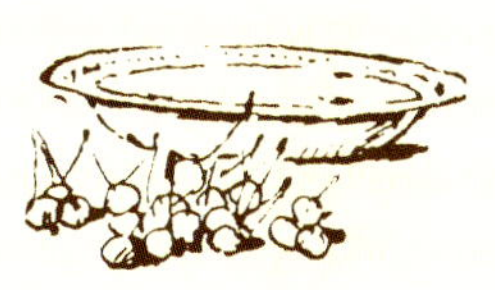

The Death of Cock Robin

The Death and Burial of Cock Robin.

WHO killed Cock Robin?
"I," said the Sparrow,
"With my bow and arrow,
I killed Cock Robin."

This is the Sparrow,
With his bow and arrow.

Who saw him die?
"I," said the Fly,
"With my little eye,
And I saw him die."

This is the little Fly,
Who saw Cock Robin die.

Who caught his blood?
"I," said the Fish,
"With my little dish,
And I caught his blood."

This is the Fish
That held the dish.

Who made his shroud?
"I," said the Beetle,
"With my little needle,
And I made his shroud."

This is the Beetle,
With his thread and needle.

Who shall dig his grave?
"I," said the Owl,
"With my spade and show'l,
And I'll dig his grave."

This is the Owl,
With his spade and show'l.

Who'll be the parson?
"I," said the Rook,
"With my little book,
And I'll be the parson."

This is the Rook,
Reading the book.

Who'll be the clerk?
"I," said the Lark,
"If it's not in the dark,
And I'll be the clerk."

This is the clerk,
Saying "Amen" like a clerk.

"Who'll carry him to the grave?
"I," said the Kite,
"If 'tis not in the night,
And I'll carry him to his grave."

This is the Kite,
About to take flight.

Who'll carry the link?
"I," said the Linnet,
"I'll fetch it in a minute,
And I'll carry the link."

This is the Linnet,
And a link with fire in it.

Who'll be the chief mourner?
"I," said the Dove,
"I mourn for my love,
And I'll be chief mourner."

This is the Dove,
Who Cock Robin did love.

Who'll sing a psalm?
"I," said the Thrush,
As she sat in a bush,
"And I'll sing a psalm."

This is the Thrush,
Singing psalms from a bush.

And who'll toll the bell?
"I," said the Bull,
"Because I can pull;"
And so, Cock Robin,
    farewell.

Sing, Sing! What Shall I Sing?

SING, sing! what shall I sing?
The cat has eat the pudding-string !
Do, do! what shall I do?
The cat has bit it quite in two.

Pease-pudding Hot.

PEASE-PUDDING hot,
   Pease-pudding cold,
Pease-pudding in the pot,
   Nine days old.

Some like it hot,
   Some like it cold,
Some like it in the pot,
   Nine days old.

Peter, Peter, Pumpkin-eater.

PETER, Peter, pumpkin-eater,
Had a wife, and couldn't keep her;
He put her in a pumpkin-shell,
And there he kept her very well.

Peter, Peter, pumpkin-eater,
Had another and didn't love her;
Peter learned to read and spell,
And then he loved her very well.

H

EY! diddle, diddle,
The cat and the fiddle,
The cow jumped
over the moon;
The little dog laughed
to see such sport,
And the dish ran away
with the spoon.

As I Was Going o'er Westminster Bridge.

As I was going o'er Westminster Bridge,
I met with a Westminster scholar;
He pulled off his cap an' drew off his glove,
And wished me a very good morrow.
What is his name?

Margery Mutton-pie.

MARGERY MUTTON-PIE and Johnny Bo-peep,
They met together in Gracechurch-street;
In and out, in and out, over the way,
Oh! says Johnny, 'tis chop-nose day.

Simple Simon Met a Pie-man.

SIMPLE Simon met a pieman
  Going to the fair;
Says Simple Simon to the pieman,
  "Let me taste your ware."

Says the pieman to Simple Simon,
  "Show me first your penny;"
Says Simple Simon to the pieman,
  "Indeed I have not any."

Simple Simon went a-fishing
  For to catch a whale;

All the water he had got
Was in his mother's pail.

Simple Simon went to look
If plums grew on a thistle;
He pricked his fingers very much,
Which made poor Simon whistle.

There Was a Little Girl.

THERE was a little girl
   Who wore a little hood,
And a curl down the middle
   of her forehead;
when she was good,
   She was very, very good,
But when she was bad,
   she was horrid.

Curly Locks! Curly Locks!.

CURLY locks! curly locks!
   Wilt thou be mine?
Thou shalt not wash dishes,
   Nor yet feed the swine;
But sit on a cushion
   And sew a fine seam,
And feed upon strawberries,
   sugar, and cream!

Over the Water.

OVER the water and over the lea,
And over the water to Charley.
Charley loves good ale and wine,
And Charley loves good brandy,
And Charley loves a pretty girl,
As sweet as sugar-candy.

Over the water and over the sea,
And over the water to Charley.
I'll have none of your nasty beef,
Nor I'll have none of your barley;
But I'll have some of your very best flour,
To make a white cake for my Charley.

Pussy-cat Ate the Dumplings.

PUSSY-CAT ate the dumplings, the dumplings,
Pussy-cat ate the dumplings.
　　Mamma stood by,
　　And cried, "Oh, fie!
Why did you eat the dumplings?"

The Girl in the Lane.

THE girl in the lane, that couldn't speak plain,
　　Cried, "Gobble, gobble, gobble";
The man on the hill, that couldn't stand still,
　　Went hobble hobble hobble.

Little Betty Blue.

LITTLE Betty Blue
   Lost her holiday shoe;
What can little Betty do?
   Give her another
   To match the other,
And then she may walk in two.

1, 2, 3, 4, 5.

1, 2, 3, 4, 5!
   I caught a hare alive;
6, 7, 8, 9, 10!
   I let her go again.

London Bridge is Broken Down.

LONDON Bridge is broken down,
    Dance o'er my lady Lee;
London Bridge is broken down,
    With a gay lady.

How shall we build it up again?
    Dance o'er my lady Lee;
How shall we build it up again'
    With a gay lady.

Silver and gold will be stole away,
    Dance o'er my lady Lee;
Silver and gold will be stole away,
    With a gay lady.

Build it up again with iron and steel,
    Dance o'er my lady Lee;
Build it up with iron and steel,
    With a gay lady.

Iron and steel will bend and bow,
    Dance o'er my lady Lee;
Iron and steel will bend and bow,
    With a gay lady.

Build it up with wood and clay,
    Dance o'er my lady Lee:
Build it up with wood and clay,
    With a gay lady.

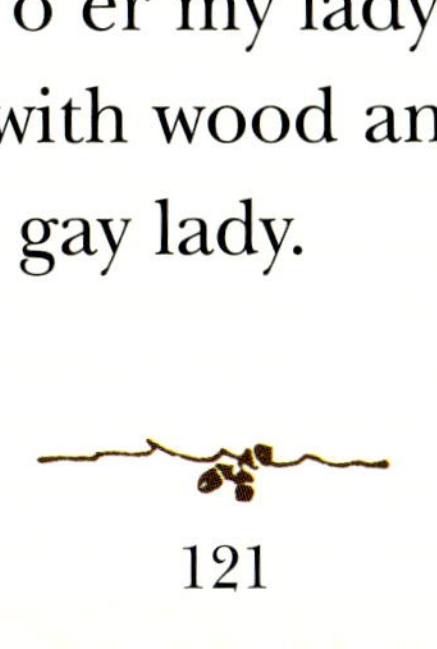

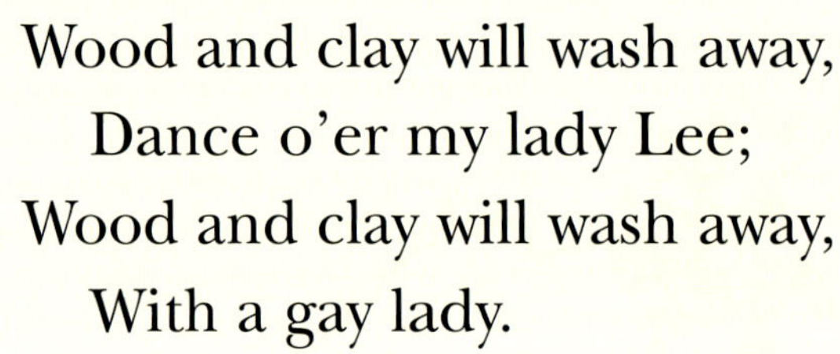

Wood and clay will wash away,
Dance o'er my lady Lee;
Wood and clay will wash away,
With a gay lady.

Build it up with stone so strong,
Dance o'er my lady Lee;
Huzza! 'twill last for ages long,
With a gay lady.

See a Pin and Pick it Up.

SEE a pin and pick it up,
All the day you'll have good luck;
See a pin and let it lay,
Bad luck you'll have all the day!

Pussy-Cat, Wussy Cat.

PUSSY CAT, wussy-cat, with a white foot,
When is your wedding? for I'll come to't.
The beer's to brew, the bread's to bake,
Pussy-cat, pussy-cat, don't be too late.

The Man in the Wilderness.

THE man in the wilderness asked me,
How many strawberries grew in the sea.
I answered him, as I thought good,
As many red herrings as grow in the wood

Doctor Foster Went to Gloucester.

DOCTOR FOSTER went to Gloucester,
  In a shower of rain;
He stepped into a puddle up to his middle,
  And never went there again.

Bow, Wow, Wow.

Bow, wow, wow,
whose dog art thou?
Little Tom Tinker's dog,
Bow, wow, wow.

I Had a Little Pony.

I HAD a little pony,
   His name was Dapple-gray;
I lent him to a lady,
   To ride a mile away;

She whipped him, she slashed him,
   She rode him through the mire;
I would not lend my pony now
   For all the lady's hire.